How Things Work:
Hot Air
Balloons

by Joanne Mattern and Blair Rainsford

Content Consultant

Nanci R. Vargus, Ed.D.
Professor Emeritus, University of Indianapolis

Reading Consultant

Jeanne M. Clidas, Ph.D.
Reading Specialist

Children's Press®
An Imprint of Scholastic Inc.

Library of Congress Cataloging-in-Publication Data
Mattern, Joanne, 1963- author.
  Hot air balloons / by Joanne Mattern.
     pages cm. -- (Rookie read-about science. How things work)
  Summary: "Introduces the reader to hot air balloons."-- Provided by publisher.
  ISBN 978-0-531-21370-4 (library binding) -- ISBN 978-0-531-21458-9 (pbk.)
  1. Hot air balloons--Juvenile literature. I. Title.

  TL638.M38 2016
  629.133'22--dc23   2015018066

Produced by Spooky Cheetah Press
Design by Keith Plechaty

© 2016 by Scholastic Inc.

Printed in China 62

SCHOLASTIC, CHILDREN'S PRESS, ROOKIE READ-ABOUT®, and associated logos are trademarks and/or registered trademarks of Scholastic Inc.

1 2 3 4 5 6 7 8 9 10 R 25 24 23 22 21 20 19 18 17 16

Photographs ©: cover: Steve Vidler/Superstock, Inc.; 3 top left: Manamana/Shutterstock, Inc.; 3 top right: Andrew Jaffee/Dreamstime; 3 bottom: Mariusz Blach/Dreamstime; 4: Steve Krull/iStockphoto; 7: Pink Sun Media/Alamy Images; 8: Carl & Ann Purcell/Corbis Images; 11: Anne Power/Dreamstime; 12: Westend61/Getty Images; 15: Anne-Marie Palmer/Alamy Images; 16: Denis Balibouse/Reuters/Landov; 21: Mike Kemp/Media Bakery; 21 background: graph/Shutterstock, Inc.; 22: Larry Lee/Larry Lee Photography/Corbis Images; 24, 25: Vladyslav Danilin/Shutterstock, Inc.; 26 left: topseller/Shutterstock, Inc.; 26 right: Patrick Foto/Shutterstock, Inc.; 26 background, 27 background: Vladimir Melnikov/Shutterstock, Inc.; 26 ropes, 27 ropes: Evgeny Karandaev/Shutterstock, Inc.; 27 left: Brandon Bourdages/Shutterstock, Inc.; 27 right: Silhouette Lover/Shutterstock, Inc.; 30 background: Paul_K/Shutterstock, Inc.; 30 left: Shamleen/Shutterstock, Inc.; 30 center left: nitinut380/Shutterstock, Inc.; 30 center right: Jonathan Larsen/Diadem Images/Alamy Images; 30 right: Henryk Sadura/Shutterstock, Inc.; 31 top: Denis Balibouse/Reuters/Landov; 31 center: Carl & Ann Purcell/Corbis Images; 31 bottom: imageBroker/Superstock, Inc.

Illustrations by Jeffrey Chandler/Art Gecko Studios!

Table of Contents

Time for a Hot Air Balloon Ride!

Hot air balloons can float thousands of feet in the air. They do not need big engines to fly, the way planes and helicopters do. All these balloons need is hot air!

A hot air balloon ride starts on Earth. The balloon is crumpled up on the ground. It looks like a birthday balloon that has not been blown up yet. How will it get into the sky?

Liftoff!

First, the hot air balloon **pilot** and
his helpers turn on a big fan.
The fan **inflates** the balloon. That
means it fills the balloon with air.
But the inflated balloon is still on
the ground.

Next, the pilot does something really surprising. He turns on a **burner** and starts a fire! It sends a flame into the balloon. The flame can shoot up to 30 feet (9 meters) high.

The fire heats up the air inside the balloon. Soon, the air in the balloon is much hotter than the air outside the balloon. Hot air is lighter than cold air. So the hot air in the balloon makes it rise into the sky.

High in the Sky

There is no steering wheel on a hot air balloon. The pilot uses the wind and the balloon's burners to change direction.

How does that work? The wind might be blowing one way, but the pilot wants to go the opposite way. So the pilot turns the flame higher.

The balloon goes up higher in the sky. Here, the wind is blowing in the opposite direction. The pilot can go where she wants now!

Back to Earth

At last, it is time to land. The pilot pulls on a rope. The rope pulls on a flap. This opens a hole at the top of the balloon. Some of the hot air in the balloon goes out the hole.

The air inside the balloon gets cooler and heavier. The balloon sinks down and down. The wind moves the balloon through the sky.

flap

Hot air balloons do not land in the same place where they took off. The pilot uses a radio to talk to his **crew** on the ground. He tells them which way the balloon is blowing.

The crew drives a truck to meet the balloon. They use a rope to help pull it to the ground.

The balloon lands gently on the ground. The sky-high ride is over!

The balloon uses simple science to soar. Look at all the parts that let the hot air balloon float into the sky.

19

So Many Balloons!

How is a hot air balloon different from other balloons?

Some balloons are filled with a gas called helium. Helium is lighter than air. It makes balloons float. You have to hold on tightly to helium balloons. They will fly away the second you let go!

The blimp is filled with helium.

The pilot and passengers ride in the gondola (GON-duh-luh).

engine

A blimp is a lighter-than-air vehicle. It is filled with helium. That makes it float. The helium also helps the blimp keep its shape.

A blimp has an engine. It is steered by a pilot.

A hot air balloon has no engine. The pilot rides the wind to move the balloon along.

Would you like to be thousands of feet high in the sky, standing in a basket, drifting along?

The first hot air balloon ride takes place in France. The balloon is filled with hot air from a fire on the ground.

Ed Yost is the first person to use an on-board burner to fly a hot air balloon.

1800

1850

1783

The first around-the-world trip in a hot air balloon takes place.

The highest balloon flight ever takes place—12 miles (19 kilometers) above Earth.

1900   1950   2000

1960   1999   2005

27

Super Science

Ask an adult for help. Do not attempt this science experiment on your own!

Hot air balloons work because hot air is lighter than cold air. You can see how the science works in this simple experiment.

You Will Need: Piece of paper, pencil, scissors, tape, lamp

1.
Draw a spiral on the piece of paper. Cut out the spiral.

2.
Tape the thread to the top of the paper spiral.

Take the cover off the lamp and let the bulb heat up.

Hold the paper spiral above the lightbulb. What happens?

Why This Works:

The heat from the lightbulb warms the air above it. As the air heats up, it rises. The movement of the air causes the spiral to spin.

That's Amazing!

A lot of hot air balloons are round. But some are made in different shapes. You can see lots of different types at a hot air balloon festival.

At a festival, pilots gather to fill the sky with beautiful balloons. Sometimes, the pilots play games in the sky. They try to drop a beanbag on a small target on the ground below. It is not easy to hit the target from so high up!

gremlin

Darth Vader

birds on a tree

scarecrow

Glossary

burner (BUR-nur): part of a hot air balloon where flames are produced

crew (KROO): team of people who work together

inflates (in-FLAYTS): makes something expand by blowing air into it

pilot (PYE-luht): person who flies a balloon or plane

Index

Facts for Now

Visit this Scholastic Web site for more information
on hot air balloons:
www.factsfornow.scholastic.com
Enter the keywords **Hot Air Balloons**

About the Author

Joanne Mattern is the author of many nonfiction books for children. Science is one of her favorite subjects to write about! Blair Rainsford lives in Brooklyn, New York, and is the editor of *Scholastic News Edition 2*.